THE HISPANIC INFLUENCE IN THE UNITED STATES

LATINOS
IN AMERICAN HISTORY

DOLORES HUERTA

BY REBECCA THATCHER MURCIA

Mitchell Lane
PUBLISHERS

P.O. Box 196
Hockessin, Delaware 19707

THE HISPANIC INFLUENCE IN THE UNITED STATES

LATINOS
IN AMERICAN HISTORY

OTHER TITLES IN THE SERIES

Visit us on the web: www.mitchelllane.com
Comments? email us: mitchelllane@mitchelllane.com

THE HISPANIC INFLUENCE IN THE UNITED STATES

LATIN?S
IN AMERICAN HISTORY

DOLORES
HUERTA

BY REBECCA THATCHER MURCIA

Mitchell Lane
PUBLISHERS

Copyright © 2003 by Mitchell Lane Publishers, Inc. All rights reserved. No part of this book may be reproduced without written permission from the publisher. Printed and bound in the United States of America.

Printing   2   3   4   5   6   7   8

Library of Congress Cataloging-in-Publication Data

Murcia, Rebecca Thatcher, 1962-
        Dolores Huerta/Rebecca Thatcher Murcia.
            p. cm. — (Latinos in American history)
        Summary: Biography of Dolores Huerta, who along with Cesar Chavez, established a union to protect the rights of farm workers.
        Includes bibliographical references (p.) and index.
        ISBN 1-58415-155-2 (lib bdg.)
        1. Huerta, Dolores, 1930—Juvenile literature. 2. Women labor leaders—United States—Biography—Juvenile literature. 3. Mexican American migrant agricultural laborers—Biography—Juvenile literature. 4. Migrant agricultural laborers—Labor unions—United States—History—Juvenile literature. 5. United Farm Workers— History—Juvenile literature. [1. Huerta, Dolores, 1930-. 2. Labor leaders. 3. United Farm Workers—History. 4. Mexican Americans—Biography. 5. Women—Biography. 6. Migrant labor.] I. Title. II. Series.
        HD6509.H84 M87 2002
        331.4'7813'092—dc21   2002013201

ABOUT THE AUTHOR: Rebecca Thatcher Murcia grew up in Garrison, New York. Her family participated in the grape boycott organized by Dolores Huerta and the United Farm Workers. She remembers explaining the reasons for the boycott to her fellow elementary school students. Murcia graduated from the University of Massachusetts at Amherst and two years later went to live and work in Brownsville, on the southern tip of Texas and the border with Mexico. She was a reporter at the *Brownsville Herald* and at the *Austin American-Statesman* for 12 years, often covering immigration issues. In 2000, Murcia, her husband, a native of Colombia, and their two boys moved to Akron, Pennsylvania, where she works as a writer, coaches her sons' soccer teams, and makes sure they remain bilingual in Spanish and English.

PHOTO CREDITS: Cover: Corbis; pp. 6, 8, 10, 14, 21, 24, 29, 32, 34, Wayne State University/Walter P. Reuther Library; pp. 36, 40 AP Photo.

PUBLISHER'S NOTE: This story is based on the author's extensive research, which she believes to be accurate. This story has not been authorized, nor endorsed by Dolores Huerta. Many of the photos in this book were taken in black and white. Some have been hand-colored for visual effect and might not necessarily reflect the original colors at the time.

CONTENTS

CHAPTER 1

CHAPTER 2

CHAPTER 3

CHAPTER 4

CHAPTER 5

CHAPTER 6

CHAPTER 7

Both Cesar Chavez and Dolores Huerta worked their entire lives to improve the working conditions for farm workers throughout the United States. For years, farm workers toiled in the hot sun in substandard conditions and for less than a livable wage. Chavez and Huerta founded the Farm Workers Association in 1962 to help the farm workers unite and bargain for better wages and benefits. Forty years after their first collective voices were heard, there is improvement, but the struggle continues.

A VICTORY FOR FARM WORKERS

CHAPTER 1

Dolores Huerta had worked all day and most of the night. She was the main speaker for a group of farm workers who were struggling for better pay and working conditions as they harvested the lettuce and other vegetables Americans eat.

She and the workers from a large lettuce farm near Salinas, California, talked for hours in a cold lunchroom with owners of the company. The workers wanted more money. They also wanted to be treated more respectfully by the owners of the farms. For years they had endured having to work with crops that had been sprayed by toxic pesticides. They had also sweated under the hot sun without drinking water or toilets. And finally, they were looking forward to signing a union contract that would provide them with benefits such as health insurance and money for retirement.

Farm workers had always worked very hard for low pay. They often traveled all across California and to other states, following the harvest and living in poor work camps, unable to find or afford decent housing. Ever since California agriculture grew big in the early 1900s, it had been like that, and nobody had been able to change it.

But Cesar Chavez, a former farm worker, and Dolores Huerta had been leading farm workers in a united effort to improve their lives for eight years. Chavez became a famous public leader of the United Farm Workers. Dolores Huerta, although not as well known, was also indispensable. She was the first vice president, the lobbyist, and the negotiator, and she worked closely with Chavez to develop the union's philosophy of nonviolence.

The workers had suffered many setbacks, but in August of 1970, a major victory was close at hand. The owners of the lettuce farm had agreed to meet with Huerta and the workers to write a contract. Many farm owners refused to even

Dolores Huerta, foreground, in the 1970s. Dolores is a tireless crusader. She has been leading marches and campaigning for change since the 1950s.

meet with the union. It was encouraging to be talking with the company owners, but it was hard to persuade them to pay the workers more.

Huerta expressed her frustration with the proposed 37 cents an hour increase for the workers, who had to bend double to harvest the low-lying lettuce. "When I think of the pain, to see those people bent over like angle worms for $1.97 an hour, it makes me sick," she said about the proposed wage. (The federal minimum wage at the time was $1.60 an hour.)

At two A.M., almost everybody in the room was tired. One of the company owners complained about how the extended talks seemed almost useless. But Huerta, who had become known as a tough and tireless negotiator, was still full of energy.

She responded without sympathy for the weary owner of the lettuce farm. "We're going for a better way of life for the farm workers," she said.

Little by little the farm owners proposed pay that was more acceptable to the workers. At four-thirty A.M. they decided to rest until ten the next morning. They continued talking that day and the next.

Finally they came to an agreement. About a thousand workers on the large farm would receive $2.10 an hour. They would also have new rules to protect them from pesticides, a hiring hall to make it more convenient to get a job, and benefits such as health insurance and money for retirement.

It was one of the sweet moments in Dolores Huerta's long effort to improve the lives of farm workers. Years of work led up to the victory. Huerta would continue for many years after to bring changes to the lives of those whose back-breaking labor brings in the harvest, year after year. ■

Dolores Huerta was raised to believe that men and women should be equal. Though her father and mother divorced, she stayed in contact with her father, who was also a unionist and eventually served in the state legislature of New Mexico. As a high school student, Huerta showed talent for organizing and concern for those around her. She became aware of the farm workers' hard lives when they sometimes stayed at a hotel that Huerta helped her mother run during World War II.

A HERO IS BORN

The town of Dawson, high in the Sangre de Cristo Mountains of northern New Mexico, is now a ghost town. But in 1930 it was alive with activity and boasted a large coal mine, a hotel, a hospital, and a bowling alley. Dolores Fernandez was born there on April 10, 1930.

Dolores was born during a hard time in American history. The Great Depression had started the year before with the stock market crash. Many people had lost their jobs and were forced to wander the country in search of work. Others turned to selling in the streets or begging.

Dolores' father, Juan Fernandez, worked in the coal mines. Mining coal is difficult, dirty, and dangerous work. Juan Fernandez believed the miners should have a union. Workers did not legally have the right to organize unions in those days, and Fernandez was fired. He became a migrant worker, following the beet harvest to Wyoming and Nebraska.

Dolores' mother, Alicia Fernandez, was a strong-willed, determined woman who believed that women and men should be treated equally. Dolores' parents divorced when Dolores was young, and her mother took Dolores and her two brothers and two sisters to live in Stockton, California.

Stockton is in the agriculturally rich San Joaquin Valley of North Central California. Alicia Fernandez worked hard there and made sure that her children were active in the community. After working at a canning factory and as a waitress, Alicia Fernandez became the owner of a 70-room hotel. The United States had entered World War II after Japan bombed Pearl Harbor, Hawaii, and over 120,000 Japanese Americans, including the owners of the hotel, were locked up in internment camps. Fernandez had been a worker at the hotel and she was left with it after the owners were sent to the camps.

Alicia Fernandez was a good businesswoman, and all of her children helped her run the hotel. While working there, Dolores saw how difficult life was for the migrant workers who picked the crops at farms near the hotel. So many American men had gone off to fight the war that the government gave the farm owners special permission to bring in workers from Mexico. It was called the bracero program, for the Spanish word for "day laborer." The problem was that the growers paid the Mexican workers poorly, and the low bracero wages pushed down the salaries of the local workers.

Sometimes the renters at the hotel would pay with rejected fruits and vegetables the growers let them have. Others would not be able to pay. One day an old man came to pay Dolores' mother with the only dollar he had. Tears rolled slowly down his cheeks. Dolores' mother asked the man what was wrong. He said he had worked all week and had almost nothing to show for it.

Alicia Fernandez treated the workers well and taught her children the importance of helping others. She believed strongly in helping the poor, without boasting about it or expecting anything in return. She also believed strongly in treating all her children equally. The boys and the girls worked equally hard in her home. Unlike girls in some other Mexican American homes, Dolores never had to do chores that her brothers did not have to do, like iron shirts or cook.

Dolores loved to dance. She studied many different kinds of dance and sometimes thought she would grow up to be a professional dancer. She enjoyed high school and continued to be active in her community. But it was in high school that Dolores first felt the sting of racial discrimination. Discrimination means treating somebody badly because of his race or religion. Though it still exists today, it is now illegal for employers or businesses to discriminate. In those days it was legal and common.

"It didn't matter whether your grades were good or not," Dolores said in a film about Hispanic women. "If you were black or brown, you got treated differently."

Dolores' high school announced a campaign to sell war bonds, certificates that promised the buyer the return of their money, plus interest, after the war. The student who sold the most war bonds would win a trophy, according to the school. Dolores sold the most bonds, but she was never awarded the trophy. She believed that the school leaders did not want to give the trophy to a Mexican American.

She also persuaded some business owners to donate a jukebox and Ping-Pong tables so that she and other teenagers would have some place to go after school. Youths of many different backgrounds, including African American, Latino, white, and Filipino, came. But the gathering of such a diverse group of youths made the police uncomfortable, and they turned off the jukebox.■

Dolores, right, sits among the farm workers and talks about their rights. She spent countless hours in the fields with the farm workers convincing them of their self-worth. She refused to allow the growers to take advantage of the workers, most of whom performed back-breaking work day after day with little or nothing to show for it at the end of the week.

THE ORGANIZER

CHAPTER 3

While Dolores did not spend hours in the fields like the children of many migrant farm workers, she did learn the hard work of fruit processing during school vacations. She found work in an apricot-packing shed, where she stood for eight hours a day, carefully but speedily cutting apricots in half with a sharp knife.

When Dolores was only 18, she married her first husband, Ralph Head. They soon became parents of two girls, Celeste and Lori. Dolores worked in a sheriff's office as a secretary, and she ran a grocery store. Her marriage to Head did not last. They divorced and Dolores' mother took care of her daughters while she went to college to become a teacher.

Dolores graduated from what is now San Joaquin Delta College in 1955. The United States was prosperous, and minorities, especially African Americans, were slowly beginning to rise up against discrimination and prejudice. They wanted a voice in the American government so that they could fight for better services and schools.

Many African Americans and Mexican Americans fought in World War II to free Europe and Asia from racist military domination. When they returned from the war, they began to question the discrimination they found in their own country.

But the 1950s were also the time of McCarthyism, when anyone who spoke out in favor of equal rights risked being accused of being a communist. Senator Joseph McCarthy held frightening hearings in which political activists were required to disclose whether they were communists and whether they knew any communists. Some refused to speak to his committee and faced harsh consequences. Many lost their jobs.

Fred Ross Sr., who had long been dedicated to helping people help themselves, was working to channel people's anger and desire for change through the Community Services Organization (CSO). The CSO's goal was to get people involved in changing their own schools and communities. CSO organizers like Ross believed that people needed to register to vote and organize group actions so that government officials would recognize their needs and treat them better.

When Ross came to Stockton, he heard that Dolores was an active, well-spoken young mother who cared about improving people's lives. Dolores was thin and short, with high cheekbones that reflected her father's Native American heritage. She had shiny black hair. "Her tongue moved as swiftly as her mind, and both left most other mortals in their wake," writer Jacques Levy recalls in *Cesar Chavez: Autobiography of La Causa.*

Ross immediately wanted to recruit Dolores, but she was at first concerned that he was a communist. After she checked with the Federal Bureau of Investigation (FBI) to make sure he was not a communist, she found Ross and the CSO compelling. Ross talked to her and other potential volunteers about how the CSO in Los Angeles had been able to get a health clinic built and forced the police to treat Mexican Americans better. "If I hadn't met Fred Ross then, I don't know if I ever would have been organizing," Dolores told *The Nation* in February 1974. "People don't realize their own worth, and I wouldn't have realized what I could do unless someone had shown faith in me. At that time we were organizing against racial discrimination. . . . I had taken the status quo for granted. But Fred said it could change. So I started working."

In the CSO, Dolores met Ventura Huerta. They were married, and Dolores, who has always loved babies, became pregnant again. Many women find being pregnant tiresome and stressful. But Huerta said being pregnant actually gave her more energy. She had five children with Ventura Huerta: Fidel, Emilio, Vincent, Alicia, and Angela. She loved her children, but she became more and more committed to her work with the CSO. She traveled all over the state organizing voter registration drives. In 1961 the CSO sent her and her family to Sacramento, the capital of California, to lobby the legislature. *Lobby* means to meet with lawmakers to persuade them to pass laws.

Huerta had never been a lobbyist. She had left her second husband and he was battling her in court for custody of their five children. Dolores was torn between fighting to keep her children and working to persuade the legislature to pass needed laws. She was raised in the Catholic Church, so she went to a church and prayed. After praying, she was convinced she needed to push for the new laws, and that if she were successful, the custody battle with her husband would also work out. And that was what happened. All 15 bills aimed at protecting the rights of Spanish-speakers and immigrants passed and became law. Dolores also kept custody of all of her children except Fidel, who lived with his father for a while before returning to his mother.

Huerta met Cesar Chavez when they were both fairly new to the CSO. Chavez was quiet and shy, and at first Huerta did not pay very much attention to him. But as they worked together, Huerta realized that Chavez was a talented organizer who cared deeply about farm workers.

Chavez was born on an 80-acre farm near Yuma, Arizona. He worked with his father, but he also had time to play and ride horses. His grandfather had built a large, adobe-walled home that remained cool even in the hot Arizona summers.

His family lost the farm in 1937, after drought and the Great Depression put his father in debt to the county tax office. Other farmers in the area received loans to keep their farms, but Cesar Chavez's father was denied a loan, and Cesar and his family had to abandon the farm they loved.

The Chavez family was forced to pack whatever they could into their old car and go west to become migrant workers. For years they followed the crops, picking cotton, grapes, and vegetables. Cesar went from the happy life of a farmer's son to helping his family barely scrape by as migrant farm workers.

After Chavez served in the U.S. Navy in World War II, he settled in San Jose, California. It was there that Fred Ross persuaded him to join the CSO. Ross taught Chavez and Huerta how to build an activist organization. They learned how to hold meetings, to listen carefully to people, and to speak before large audiences.

When they decided to begin a new effort to form a farm workers union, they were ready.

Being a leader in the CSO taught Huerta that if a group of people worked together, they could win a change. She had seen it happen over and over again. But the CSO focused mostly on city dwellers. Dolores believed that farm workers needed their own, separate organization.

While most Americans took tap water and indoor bathrooms for granted in 1960, a state survey of 100 farm worker families showed that the majority did not have running water in their homes and that one-third of them used privies, or outdoor toilets.

The AFL-CIO, the organization that represents most American unions, sent organizers to California in 1959 to start a farm workers union. Huerta had been pleased to see an effort being made to help farm workers and agreed to help. But the organizers did not speak Spanish and knew little about farm labor. They made a big mistake. They became friendly with farm labor contractors. Farm workers often dislike farm labor contractors because they charge farm workers to bring them to the farms, then they take a commission from the workers' earnings. If union organizers used the contractors to sign the workers up for the union, the union would never win the trust of the workers, Huerta thought.

When Huerta saw the organizers meeting with farm labor contractors, she thought their effort was doomed and resigned. She and Cesar Chavez agreed that farm workers had to be convinced that joining a union was right, not forced to join by a boss or a contractor. A farm workers union needed to be democratic, or run by the workers themselves.

Chavez decided to ask the CSO to sponsor a farm worker organizing project. A few leaders of the CSO agreed with Chavez, and they expected everyone else to agree. But when all the CSO leaders met in Calexico, California, in the spring of 1962, they voted not to support Chavez's project. Huerta was disappointed, but she did not expect what happened next. "I resign," Chavez announced. Huerta cried, but in her heart she knew Chavez was making the right decision. She decided to follow him.

"I quit the CSO because I couldn't stand seeing kids coming to class hungry and needing shoes," she said in an interview with *The Progressive* in September 2000. "I thought I could do more by organizing farm workers than trying to teach their hungry children."

But it was also a scary decision. Huerta had seven children and Chavez had eight. Huerta told Chavez she needed to be able to feed her children. Chavez told her not to worry. "I gave up my job as a schoolteacher to organize farm workers without knowing where my next meal was coming from. At the time I had seven kids and I was a single mother," Huerta said years later in a video interview. "But I just knew it could happen."

Huerta began organizing the union in the Stockton area, and Chavez began in Delano. Their tactics were simple at first. They did not call the project a union. They called it the Farm Workers Association because they did not want people to think the union was going to go on strike right away. They gave people a form to fill out, asking their name, address, and what they thought was a fair wage. When people returned the form, they met with them to explain the goals of the new organization.

By September 1962 they were ready to call a founding convention. After months of quiet conversations and house meetings, it was time to call all the members together and make their goals public. Huerta paced nervously around the old movie theater they had rented in Fresno. She wanted everything to go right at the important meeting. She made sure snacks were ready at the back of the hall. She checked the seats, hoping they would all be filled.

Finally the farm workers began filing in. Many still had their work clothes on. Some held babies as they chatted excitedly about their hopes for the new organization. Some remembered how farm workers had been beaten and arrested for past attempts to form a union. Everybody cheered as the speeches began. The convention voted to push politicians to set a $1.50-an-hour minimum wage (up from $1.15), to advocate the right of farm workers to bargain collectively with farm owners, and to start an insurance program and a credit union. They also agreed to collect $3.50 a month in dues. Chavez was elected president and Huerta was elected vice president.

The meeting ended on an exciting note, with Chavez's cousin, Manuel Chavez, unveiling a banner for the union. The large red flag had a white circle in the center with a

This now-famous photograph was taken at the founding convention of the NFWA on September 30, 1962. From left to right: José Martinez, Dolores Huerta, Tony Orendain, and Cesar Chavez.

black eagle in the middle of it. People cheered, stamped their feet, and shouted their support. "When that damn eagle flies, the problems of the farm workers will be solved!" Manuel Chavez cried.

The convention was an exciting high point in the early days of the new union, but difficult days followed. Chavez had hoped to be able to pay Huerta and himself a small salary from the union dues, but many members didn't pay their dues. Cesar Chavez and his wife, Helen Chavez, returned to picking cotton to support their family. Huerta was able to scrape by on some child support checks from her former husbands, and a little unemployment insurance. She pressed politicians in Sacramento to support the minimum wage hike and other proposals supported by the farm workers. One lawmaker was so impressed with her that he tried to get her to work for the government. It was a tempting offer that would have given her a steady income and money to support her family more comfortably.

But Huerta always believed that she and her family had to sacrifice so that farm workers could have better lives. She would pack all seven of her children in the car and drive around to farm worker communities, working to persuade people to join the union. She declined the lawmaker's offer.

In 1964, President Lyndon Johnson was expanding the United States' involvement in the Vietnam War. He was also promising a new fight against poverty in the United States. African Americans and Mexican Americans were becoming more and more inclined to insist on their rights and fight against the discrimination that was so common. Huerta moved to Delano to be closer to the union headquarters Chavez was setting up. They wanted to make sure the union was large and had enough money before they directly challenged any growers by calling a strike.

But sometimes events force people to act. In the spring of 1965, a rose worker came to the union wanting to stop abuses in the rose industry in the McFarland area. Rose grafting, in which a worker inserts rosebuds into mature bushes, requires workers to kneel as their hands work at lightning speed. The workers had been promised nine dollars for each 1,000 plants, but instead they were getting only about seven dollars. Huerta and Chavez met with the grafters for several weeks, and then decided to lead a strike against the biggest company, which employed about 85 people.

None of the workers went to the rose farm on the morning of the strike, and the owners were furious. Huerta knocked on the office door at around 10:30 A.M. The manager shouted, "Get out, you Communist, get out!" according to *Cesar Chavez: Autobiography of La Causa*.

The day before the strike started, all the workers had met and sworn on a cross that they would not return until the leaders said the strike was over. However, a day or so after it began, Huerta suspected that one group of men might be heading to work. She drove a truck to their house, parked it in their driveway so that their car was blocked in, and then hid the truck keys. The workers were embarrassed and agreed to stick to their pledge. Four days later the company owner agreed to a wage hike, but the company never did allow the union to represent the workers.

Word of the successful strike spread through farm worker communities. Chavez and Huerta still thought it would be a few years before they could take on the big grape growers that surrounded Delano. They thought they needed more time to establish the union. They needed to train leaders and build a strike fund so that workers could receive money for food during the strike.

But history, as it turned out, refused to wait.■

The UFW has worked hard for many years to win contracts for workers at the Ernst & Julio Gallo Company, a large California winery. In 2000, the UFW negotiated a contract covering about 300 workers at one of the Gallo vineyards, Gallo of Sonoma.

THE CAUSE FOR GRAPES

CHAPTER 4

Pressure had been put on the growers to end the bracero program, which enabled them to bring in workers from Mexico and pay them less than local workers demanded. But in 1965 the growers won the right to continue, under the condition that they pay their workers $1.40 an hour (15 cents over federal minimum wage). When grape pickers in Southern California, many of them from the Philippines, heard that braceros were going to be paid more than local workers, they went on strike. The strike spread north under the leadership of the Agricultural Workers Organizing Committee, the AFL-CIO–backed effort that did not originally seem well run.

Chavez and Huerta knew their union was not ready for a big strike. But they also knew they could not violate a strike that was spreading throughout the grape arbors of California.

On September 16, Mexican Independence Day, they called for a mass meeting of the union membership to decide what to do. Farm workers from far and wide crammed into Our Lady of Guadalupe Church. Chavez reminded the packed sanctuary that 155 years earlier, a famous priest had called for the liberation of Mexico. "We are engaged in another struggle for the freedom and dignity which poverty denies us," Chavez said. "But it must not be a violent struggle, even if violence is used against us. Violence can only hurt us and our cause."

Farm workers from different parts of Mexico voiced their support for the strike. One old man recalled seeing strikers killed in the 1930s, but he said the struggle must continue because farm workers had progressed so little.

When it came time to vote on the strike, it was unanimous. The workers knew their walkout would prompt a reaction from the growers and the politicians and police who supported them. But they might not have known how drastic the response would be.

After a few days to give the growers a chance to respond to their demands, the workers began picketing the farms, carrying signs and shouting at the workers who had either decided not to strike or didn't know about the strike. Sometimes cheers and applause would break out when they managed to persuade the non-strikers to walk off the job. The growers responded by threatening the picketers and spraying them with dust or pesticide.

Once Huerta grew very thirsty while leading a picket line, so she asked a female picker for a little of her water. The woman went to bring Huerta the water, but the supervisor became so angry that he kicked the water out of the woman's hands. Everyone was very upset, and the woman and all her fellow workers walked off the job.

Huerta was one of the people in charge of organizing the picket lines and deciding which farms and entrances to picket. One day when she was returning from a picket line, her car overheated. She and the other union members got out of the car and went to a nearby house to ask for water. A grower came rushing out of the house with a shotgun, which he fired over their heads.

Despite the growers' violent reactions, the two unions, which were now working together, did not give in. All through the fall and winter, they kept the strike going. They called for help from ministers and church leaders. They publicized the story as much as they could on national television and in major newspapers.

The U.S. Constitution, the law on which the U.S. government is based, says free speech is a fundamental right. Picketing along a public road is a form of free speech allowed by the Constitution. But growers would often persuade local police and judges to have the picketers, including Huerta, arrested and thrown in jail. This habit led to a famous exchange between a local sheriff and U.S. Senator Robert F. Kennedy at a hearing on the strike. The sheriff, testifying at the hearing, said he arrested picketers to prevent them from getting hurt. Kennedy was shocked at the way the sheriff violated the farm workers' rights. He told the sheriff he should read the U.S. Constitution.

The FBI was called in, not to protect the farm workers' rights, but to investigate whether the union's leaders were communists. Early in the investigation the FBI reported that the union was not led or controlled by communists, but the FBI surveillance continued for more than 10 years. In 1992 when the reports were made public under the Freedom of Information Act, they showed that agents had noticed Huerta's role in the strike. According to *The Fight in the Fields: Cesar Chavez and the Farmworkers Movement*, the FBI reported that Huerta was "the driving force on the picket lines of Delano and Tulare County and daily inspire[d] the pickets and their cause."

Although violence against the farm workers was common, Chavez later remembered how Huerta seemed to be especially good at preventing violence. "She's stopped more violence than anybody," he recalled in *Sal Si Puedes (Escape If You Can).*

By spring, the strike was still dragging on with no sign that the growers would give in. Chavez decided to lead a 300-mile march from Delano to Sacramento. The march drew supporters all along its route. El Teatro Campesino, a farm workers theater group, entertained the crowds with startling comedy about farm workers and growers. Huerta stayed in Delano to keep the picket lines going.

Toward the end the march, the first grape farmer called Chavez and offered to recognize the union and negotiate a contract. Chavez at first didn't believe the call was genuine. But it was. In Sacramento, the long march ended in a victory celebration. But a true victory was still over four long years away.

The other grape farmers did not fall into line behind the first. The largest farm, Di Giorgio Fruit Corporation, hinted that it would negotiate, but then it bused in hundreds of strikebreakers from Mexico. Finally political pressure persuaded Di Giorgio to let the workers vote on whether they wanted a union. The union won the election. Huerta negotiated a groundbreaking contract that included raises, fairer hiring practices, vacation and holiday pay, and other benefits.

Another winery gave in, and Huerta worked around the clock on yet another contract. As the blitz of negotiations wound down, Huerta fainted from exhaustion and had to be hospitalized for a few days.

In 1967 the union made tremendous strides. It had contracts covering about 5,000 workers. The leaders hoped the progress would continue. But the table grape growers discovered a way to undermine the progress. They began using labels from unionized farms on grapes from nonunion farms.

While the controversy over the fake labels raged, Senator Robert Kennedy announced that he would run for president. Huerta and Chavez were stretched to the limit, but they thought they had to help Kennedy, who had long supported the farm workers. They organized an effort to register voters and get out the vote. Kennedy won the California primary, and Huerta went with him on stage at the victory rally at the Ambassador Hotel in Los Angeles. Kennedy thanked her and Chavez for their help. He finished his speech and was whisked through the ballroom kitchen. It was there that he

Dolores believed that the only way to beat the label-switching was an industry-wide boycott of table grapes. In 1970, after seeing grape sales decline drastically, the growers gave in.

was shot. He died the next day. Kennedy's death was a huge loss, but the farm workers had little time to mourn.

Huerta believed the only way to beat the label-switching was to call an industry-wide boycott of table grapes. Though raisins, wine, and other products are made from grapes, the union leaders focused that boycott on table grapes because it was the table grape growers who they thought were taking advantage of the union. She told Chavez what she thought, and he agreed. The grape boycott, which would eventually involve about 17 million Americans, was on.

Union members were sent to cities all over the United States to organize demonstrations and promote the boycott. Huerta went to New York City. She said she remembers arriving in the city wondering how in the world she was going to stop 11 million people from buying grapes. But Americans all over the country heard the farm workers' call and began to leave the table grapes in the stores. Some stores and restaurants began refusing to sell the grapes.

In 1970, after seeing grape sales decline drastically, the growers gave in.

Huerta rushed back to California, where she negotiated about 200 three-year contracts that gave raises and new benefits to thousands and thousands of workers. Her tactics became legendary throughout the industry. She would bring workers to the sessions and have them testify about their living conditions. She always had a quick response to growers' sarcastic comments.

Huerta's relentless optimism and energy shows clearly in a film of a speech she gave to farm workers in Arizona in 1971. "We are building an organization, a union, that will make the social and economic changes to make us free men and women," she says in her clear, fluent Spanish. "And we are going to see victory soon!"

All this time Huerta was also a mother of seven children. Some of them went with her to New York City and others stayed in California with union members. They wore donated or secondhand clothes and ate donated food. She has said she often felt terrible about the sacrifices her children made so that she could lead the labor union. But she would often tell them that they had to do without so that another child would have enough to eat.

Years later, her children said it was tough and frightening at times. But Huerta and her children said they learned very important lessons by being part of such an significant movement. "Taking my kids all over the states made them lose their fear of people, of new situations," Huerta said in an interview with *The Nation* in February 1974. "My kids are totally politicized mentally and the whole idea of working without materialistic gain has made a great difference in the way they think."

But Huerta did not remain a single mother for much longer. She and Cesar Chavez's brother, Richard Chavez, fell in love. Though some sources describe him as her husband, more reliable and in-depth ones agree that they were never formally married. Dolores and Richard had four children together: Juanita, Maria Elena, Ricky, and Camilla. ◼

UFW leaders Marshall Ganz (left), Dolores Huerta (center), and Richard Chavez consider a document. By the time Richard Chavez and Dolores fell in love, Huerta's oldest daughters were grown. Richard and Dolores had four children, bringing the total of Dolores' children to 11. Huerta said her children had few toys and wore old clothes when they were growing up. But they learned a great deal as children of the union and have had a variety of different and interesting careers.

THE GROWERS' BACKLASH

I n the early 1970s Huerta and the other union leaders worked to administer their rapidly growing union. They had to oversee the retirement account and a medical benefits plan, plus teach the workers how to make sure the contracts were followed. They concentrated on the work and did not think too much about new tactics the growers might use when the contracts expired in 1973.

The Teamsters, a union mostly of truck drivers, had long been notorious for its lack of ethics and its links to organized crime. In the past, the growers had sometimes tried to use the Teamsters against the farm workers union.

Still, in 1973 Huerta and the other leaders were shocked when the growers secretly signed new contracts with the Teamsters, even though the workers had not voted to be represented by the Teamsters. Much later they would find out that President Richard Nixon, who had been elected with Teamster backing and would later resign in disgrace, had ordered government officials to back the Teamsters.

Just as before, the union sent the workers to the picket line to protest the secret contracts. They also called for a new boycott. This time, the picketers were met by Teamsters who were even more violent than previous opponents.

Juan de la Cruz, an elderly longtime union supporter, was shot and killed on the picket line. Another member was hit on the head on the street and died. Huerta and Chavez were horrified by the killings and called off the pickets. Huerta realized farm workers needed a law to protect their right to choose their own representatives for negotiations with farm owners. It should have been illegal for the growers to sign secret Teamster contracts, but it was not.

Farmworker organizers often used humor to publicize their cause and keep spirits high. In this photo, a sign plays on the word "bureau" saying, in Spanish, "Down with the farm burro (or donkey.)"

Huerta and other leaders began meeting to write a proposed law and figure out how to get it approved by the California legislature and the governor. It was a huge undertaking. The federal government's labor law specifically said it did not include farm workers. No other state had a state law protecting farm workers' rights.

But Huerta, who had worked to get laws passed in Sacramento with the CSO more than a decade earlier, pressed onward. California governor Jerry Brown signed the Agricultural Labor Relations Act on June 5, 1975. The law created a five-member board that would oversee elections and require farm owners to recognize unions that win elections. It also required farm owners to allow union organizers to meet with farm workers.

The passage of the law was a victory for the union, but it turned out that the board did not enforce the law as well as the union leaders had hoped. The board did not have enough people to investigate all the violations the union reported, and growers continued to file appeals even after the union had won elections.

Despite the obstacles, the union continued organizing and growing. A big organizing effort in the lettuce fields brought the membership up to 100,000 by 1980. Chavez and Huerta became more and more well known. They frequently traveled for speaking engagements and organizing events. Huerta remained as committed as ever to the union, but she also began to branch out as an activist.■

President Bill Clinton gave Dolores Huerta the Eleanor Roosevelt Award for Human Rights at a White House ceremony in 1999. The award was named for Eleanor Roosevelt, wife of President Franklin Delano Roosevelt, and a long-time advocate of racial and economic justice.

HUERTA AND FEMINISM

Huerta was raised to believe that women should be treated equal to men. All her life she worked as a labor organizer, a field dominated by men. But in the 1980s she saw a need to become more outspoken as a feminist.

She was watching politicians on television in 1987 when it struck her hard: As long as men were making all the decisions, women were not going to be treated equally. She joined the National Organization for Women and became more active in feminist causes.

She didn't attack union members for making sexist statements during meetings. She just counted them. At first there were many. She would add up the list and announce the total. Little by little the men began to pay attention to the way they talked. She thought more about girls and young women and the challenges they face. "We shouldn't let anybody else take control of our bodies," she said. "We want to go and cut a path for our own lives, and we shouldn't let anyone stand in our way. Women are not servants. We serve because we want to serve."

But her commitment to the union never flagged. Some of the other longtime leaders of the union left in the 1980s. Huerta said many of the people who left were tired of the low pay the union offered, but some of the people who left said it was because of Chavez's management style. Huerta herself had lots of arguments with Chavez, but she kept working.

She joined a protest outside a San Francisco hotel where Vice President George Bush was speaking in 1988. She was spreading the word about the UFW's new grape boycott, which had been called to protest the use of dangerous pesticides on table grapes.

Huerta was pressed up against a police barrier when a police officer told her to move back. She was trying to move back when he hit her in the stomach with his nightstick. The blow ruptured her spleen and fractured two ribs. At first Richard Chavez did not think she was too badly injured. But later a surgeon told him that she had almost bled to death as she waited for treatment in the hospital emergency room.

The city of San Francisco, known as a haven for liberal politics, was in an uproar over the attack. There was an investigation and Huerta filed a lawsuit. The city promised to change its crowd control methods and settled out of court with Huerta for $825,000. She planned to give the money to activist groups.

Huerta dedicated her life to building the United Farm Workers. She was there when the union needed a lobbyist. She was there when it needed a negotiator. She was ready when the union needed a spokeswoman. But she never demanded recognition for her achievements. And she often didn't receive much credit. Cesar Chavez was the union president, and, rightly or wrongly, he garnered most of the attention. Though he focused his efforts on farm workers, he became known as a national leader of Mexican Americans, just as Martin Luther King Jr. was known as a leader of African Americans.

In the 1990s Huerta began to emerge more publicly as a powerful speaker and organizer. When Cesar Chavez died in 1993, she was among the leaders who promised to keep the union going. She became even more committed to causes such as getting more women elected to public office and helping women protect their reproductive rights.

President Bill Clinton invited Huerta to the White House to receive the Eleanor Roosevelt Award for Human Rights in 1999. Clinton praised her many years of hard work and said, "Dolores, we thank you for all you have done and all you still do to promote the dignity and human rights of your family and America's family."

Meanwhile, a wave of anti-immigrant sentiment was prompting residents of her home state of California to propose laws Huerta saw as anti-immigrant and anti-Latino. Huerta and the United Farm Workers waged a tough campaign against Proposition 187. Proposition 187 said that undocumented children should not be allowed in the public schools or be given public health services. They also battled two other propositions against bilingual education and affirmative action in higher education. Despite UFW rallies, marches, and door-to-door organizing, all the propositions passed. Only Proposition 187 was ruled invalid by a federal judge.

Huerta kept working. Finally, in 1999, at the age of 69, she resigned from her position as secretary-treasurer of the union. However, she was not retiring: She wanted to be able to campaign full-time for Vice President Al Gore, who was running for president against Texas governor George W. Bush.■

United Farm Workers President Arturo Rodriguez, right, followed by UFW co-founder Dolores Huerta, lead members of the UFW as they continue their 150-mile march near Thornton, California, on August 22, 2002. The march started in Merced and ended in Sacramento where the members held a rally in an effort to persuade Governor Gray Davis to sign a bill that forced binding arbitration when contract talks fail between growers and unions. Though the binding arbitration did not become law, Davis did sign a bill calling for mediators and the Agricultural Labor Relations Board to decide on the terms of a contract when the union and the growers cannot agree.

A LEGACY OF EMPOWERMENT

Dolores worked hard on the presidential campaign, but just before the election she fell ill. Doctors discovered an opening in her aortic artery. She underwent emergency surgery. On Election Day she was still weak from surgery, but from her hospital bed she urged people to be sure to vote. She was released from the hospital only to have to return a few weeks later when she became sick with pneumonia. After she recovered from pneumonia, she resumed her schedule of organizing, speaking and—more and more frequently—receiving awards.

Mohandas Gandhi, who led India's peaceful struggle for independence from Britain, is considered the modern era's leading pioneer in promoting peaceful political change. Gandhi and other advocates of nonviolence were important examples for Huerta. Just as Huerta was inspired by leaders before her, she has inspired a subsequent generation of leaders.

As she traveled around the country, often to receive honors or to speak at a ceremony to name a school or a center after her, she continued to urge young people to fight peacefully for political change. She often said it is normal to be afraid, but that young people need to overcome their fear. On April 5, 2000, Huerta spoke at the Center for Latino and Latin American Studies at Northern Illinois University. As was her custom, she asked people to think about why they are taught to value highly paid professions like lawyers over the work of farm workers.

"Farm workers do the most sacred work of all—feeding us," Huerta said. "But they are the most ignored."

Huerta was always a fiery speaker. Toward the end of her speeches, she would call on her audiences to participate in a time-honored Latin American tradition of shouting rounds of *¡Qué viva!* with her. She would shout, for example, *"¡Qué viva Cesar Chavez!"* ("Long live Cesar Chavez!"), and the audience would respond by shouting, *"¡Qué viva!"* Then she would say, *"¡Qué viva la unión!"* and the audience would repeat, *"¡Qué viva!"* To go to a Dolores Huerta speech was not to sit quietly and listen, but to be called upon to act, to respond, and even to shout.

When activists in Las Vegas, Nevada, opened a center to help workers learn about their rights, they named it the Dolores Huerta Center for Worker Rights. The director of the center, Mayra Ocampo, knew Huerta when she was a child and her father worked with the United Farm Workers in Salinas, California. "This is someone who has dedicated all her life to the cause," Ocampo said. "We couldn't think of anyone better."

Huerta hopes to keeping working for change—for an end to poverty; for respect for workers; for equal rights for immigrants, minorities, and women—for many years. But even Huerta will eventually have to slow down. Then new generations will have her example to follow.■

CHRONOLOGY

1930   Dolores Fernandez is born in Dawson, New Mexico

1935   Moves to Stockton, California, with her mother

1948   Marries Ralph Head; they have two children

1955   Graduates from Delta Community College with a teaching degree; begins teaching and working with Community Services Organization; marries Ventura Huerta; they eventually have five children

1959   Works briefly with the AFL-CIO's farm worker organizing effort, the Agricultural Workers Organizing Committee, but resigns when she realizes its tactics are inadequate

1961   She and Ventura Huerta separate; she successfully lobbies in Sacramento for the Community Services Organization

1962   Leaves the CSO to begin organizing farm workers with Cesar Chavez

1965   With Chavez, leads the farm workers' union in its first strike

1966   Negotiates the union's first contract

1968   Goes to New York to organize the grape boycott; was with Senator Robert F. Kennedy moments before he was assassinated

1970   Juanita, the first of four children Dolores and Richard Chavez will have, is born

1975   Lobbies for the passage of the California Agricultural Labor Relations Act

1988   Is severely beaten by police at a protest in San Francisco

1993   Mourns the death of Cesar Chavez, but vows to continue his work in building the United Farm Workers

1999   Awarded the Eleanor Roosevelt Award for Human Rights by President Bill Clinton; resigns as secretary-treasurer of the United Farm Workers to campaign for Al Gore, the Democratic Party's presidential nominee

2000   Wins the Hispanic Heritage Award; undergoes open-heart surgery

2001   Honored for lifetime achievement by *Hispanic* Magazine

2002   Continues to work for change and to receive awards around the country

1905   The International Workers of the World (IWW), a small, radical union, is begun as an alternative to the mainstream labor movement

1910   A revolution and the ensuing violence in Mexico pushes thousands of Mexicans to emigrate to California

1913   Two IWW leaders are imprisoned after a fatal riot at a farm in California.

1917   World War I begins and opposition to the IWW builds. Hundreds of IWW activists are imprisoned, and the union's power begins to decline.

1934   The so-called Dust Bowl refugees, farmers from Oklahoma, Texas, and other Midwestern states, begin moving into California to work as migrant laborers after their farms are ruined by a long drought. *The Grapes of Wrath,* John Steinbeck's popular novel about the Dust Bowl refugees, raises many citizens' awareness of the conditions in the fields.

1935   President Franklin Delano Roosevelt signs the National Labor Relations Act, giving all American workers, except farm, airline, railroad, and government workers, the right to organize a union and bargain collectively with their employers.

1937   Cesar Chavez's father loses the family farm in Arizona after banks deny him a loan to pay taxes. The family goes to California to become migrant laborers.

1939   U.S. Senator Robert M. La Follette Jr., chairman of the Senate Committee on Education and Labor, begins holding hearings on the working conditions of farm workers. The committee's report details the "shocking degree of human misery" among farm workers.

1942   Powerful growers, complaining that too many workers have left the fields to serve in World War II, win the right to set up what became known as the bracero program.

1956   "Strangers in Our Fields," a report by farm labor organizer Ernesto Galarza, details widespread abuses and violations in the bracero program.

1959 The AFL-CIO sponsors the new Agricultural Workers Organizing Committee

1962 Cesar Chavez, Dolores Huerta, and others begin the Farm Workers Association, later to be known as the United Farm Workers.

1965 Thousands of grape workers in California walk off the job

1966 As the grape strike drags on without results, farm workers march 300 miles to Sacramento, the capital of California.

1968 The union calls for a widespread boycott of table grapes, sending volunteers to 40 U.S. cities to promote the boycott; Cesar Chavez fasts for 26 days

1970 After five years of strikes, marching, and boycotts, grape growers gradually begin to recognize the union.

1973 As the UFW contracts expire, many growers sign secret agreements with the Teamsters.

1975 California passes the Agricultural Labor Relations Act, which is designed to protect farm workers' right to form unions. It creates a farm labor board that will oversee elections, but the union finds that the California legislature will not give the board enough money to do its job effectively.

1980 United Farm Workers membership peaks at more than 100,000.

1982 Governor George Deukmejian, a Republican, is elected and appoints antiunion officials to the state's farm labor board. Union contracts and memberships decline.

1988 Chavez fasts for 36 days to protest the use of pesticides.

1993 Chavez dies April 23 at the age of 66.

2001 The United Farm Workers continues its effort to organize farm workers, but also branches out to organize workers at a furniture factory. Although it has helped improve the lives of thousands of farm workers, the workers continue to struggle with poor housing and working conditions.

2002 Farm labor bill in California passes that calls for mediators and the Agricultural Labor Relations Board to decide on the terms of a contract when negotiations between farm workers and growers break down. The new law takes effect on January 1, 2003 and expires in 2008. The union had pressed for binding arbitration and a permanent law, though the mediation terms are seen as a victory for the union.

FOR FURTHER READING

Anaya, Rudolfo. *An Elegy on the Death of Cesar Chavez*. El Paso, Tex.: Cinco Puntos Press, 2000.

De Ruiz, Dana Catharine, and Richard Larios. *La Causa: The Migrant Farmworkers' Story*. New York: Steck-Vaughn Company, 1993.

Drake, Susan Samuels. "Dolores Huerta." *The Progressive*, September 2000, pp. 34–38.

Felner, Julie. "Woman of the Year: Dolores Huerta." *Ms. Magazine*, January/February 1998.

Ferriss, Susan, and Ricardo Sandoval. *The Fight in the Fields: Cesar Chavez and the Farmworkers Movement*. New York: Harcourt Brace, 1997.

Levy, Jacques E. *Cesar Chavez: Autobiography of La Causa*. New York: W.W. Norton and Company, Inc., 1975.

Matthiessen, Peter. *Sal Si Puedes (Escape If You Can): Cesar Chavez and the New American Revolution*. New York: Random House, 1969.

Meister, Dick. *A Long Time Coming: The Struggle to Unionize America's Farm Workers*. New York: Macmillan Publishing Co., 1977.

Rountree, Cathleen. *On Women Turning Fifty*. San Francisco: Harper San Francisco, 1994.

Zannos, Susan. *Cesar Chavez* (A Real-Life Reader Biography). Bear, DE: Mitchell Lane Publishers, Inc. 1999.

ON THE WEB

Cesar E. Chavez Foundation
http://www.cesarechavezfoundation.org/
The United Farm Workers
http://www.ufw.org

GLOSSARY

AFL-CIO: the American Federation of Labor and Congress of Indus-
trial Organizations. The umbrella organization uniting the American
labor movement.

Bracero (bra-SAY-ro): a Mexican worker brought to the United States
by the U.S. government from 1942 to 1949.

Commission (kuh-MISH-in): a fee paid to an agent for performing a
service, such as finding a person a job.

Contract: a written agreement between two organizations or people,
usually saying how much will be paid for a product or service.

Negotiator (neh-GOH-she-ayt-er): a person who meets with others to
find a solution to a conflict.

Strike: a work stoppage with the purpose of persuading an employer to
give in to workers' demands.

Toxic (TAHKS-ik): poisonous

Union (YOUN-yun): an organization of employees that negotiates with
the employer on issues such as pay and working conditions.

INDEX